YOUNG BLACK
& ────
DANGEROUS

YOUNG BLACK
& ————
DANGEROUS

A GANGSTERS MEMOIR

LEWIS POPE

iUniverse®

YOUNG BLACK & DANGEROUS
A GANGSTERS MEMOIR

iUniverse books may be ordered through booksellers or by contacting:

iUniverse
1663 Liberty Drive
Bloomington, IN 47403
www.iuniverse.com
1-800-Authors (1-800-288-4677)

ISBN: 978-1-4917-9630-6 (sc)
ISBN: 978-1-4917-9631-3 (e)

Print information available on the last page.

iUniverse rev. date: 05/04/2016

INTRODUCTION

I was twenty years old when I wrote this book. I did not intend on publishing this at all. I left Miami and went to Los Angeles in February 2008 to pursue a better lifestyle and succeed with my rap career. I did not care about the obstacles I was about to face, I just knew in my heart that I wanted things to change for the better because nothing was happening for me in Miami. When I got to L.A. I tried to make something happen but failed, not once but twice! I was living in a motel in watts for a couple of weeks and had to leave because I was almost out of money.

I did not know anyone in L.A. And wasn't the type of person to beg or accept hand outs from people that I do not know. So I left L.A. And went to stay with my grandpa and grandma in Arizona. I had a hard time adapting to where I was because they lived in a area called Peoria which is majority rich white folks. A lot of them were old so I hardly seen them. Peoria was far from the inner city so I did not have anyone to relate to. I tried doing several different things to help the time go by but this prison like setting eventually started affecting my mind. I did not understand at that time that god was doing this to me for a reason. I had came to a crossroad in my life, and the only way to move forward was to face my demons and overcome them. I was initiated into the bloods back in Miami, and was involved in a lot of things that can ultimately alter and destroy the life that I was blessed with. This book is the written transformation that I experienced in Arizona. I hope this book gives other street souljahs insight on how they can break free from this plague that so many of us have been consumed by. One day at a time, may each one teach one. One Love

FRUSTRATED

1. Today was my first day working as a McDonald's employee. It was frustrating at first, and those demons started calling me. I wanted to break out on their ass, but I stayed humble. It is extra and extremely hard for a brother like me to keep control of myself under such buster ass conditions. After getting the hang of how they operate I handled my situation much better. I know for a fact that I need money, and a real hustler is capable of getting money legally and illegally. I must get money whichever way I can. I am trying to keep my head up, and stay as humble as possible. That doesn't mean I won't fuck a muthafucka up though.

VULNERABLE

2. All the dirt that I have done makes me feel vulnerable, and unfortunately leads to my thoughts of committing suicide. I don't know what the next day will bring, but I do know whatever it is I will be man enough to face it. Lord knows its hard out here for a young black brother. We have to work ten times as hard just to get something accomplished. I hope my brothers in heaven can see that I am trying my best to do the right thing. Where do I go from here? Do I keep straight or take another route? Life is hectic right now, but I have to do something. I refuse to be a lost soul.

SERIOUS

3. I get extremely angry when people take what I say as a joke, or don't take it serious. I am a very serious individual. I laugh but I don't joke, I am not a comedian! This is what lead to my antisocial state in the first place! I am trapped in madness and driven by hate. Only if they knew what dwells deep inside of me. If they could take a peek, I bet their laughter would cease! I cannot lie, sometimes I go overboard, but it is hard not to go overboard when you are constantly on the edge. Lord knows how hard it is to stay humble in a world filled with violence, hate, and rage.

OPERATION "SILENT BUT DEADLY"

4. I am sick and tired of people pointing their finger at me. I do what I have to, and say what I want, that's just me. I have a trick up my sleeve though. For all those who don't like what I say, I bring to them "silent but deadly"! This emerges from my soul when I feel that there is no need to talk anymore. I don't feel like I need to make any threats or explain to anyone how I feel, because they wouldn't give a shit anyway. I feel like actions are louder than words. Keep your eyes open and your mouth shut! Rules of survival are what I live and die by.

"RULES OF SURVIVAL"

1. Keep god first

2. Have faith

3. humble yourself

4. Be aware

5. Take care of your business

6. discipline!!!!!!!

7. Love and believe in yourself

8. keep your eyes and ears open and your mouth shut!

9. Move swiftly and silently. Be seen but not heard.

10. Take your time

11. Play your cards right

12. Stay focused

MENACE TO SOCIETY

6. I feel like a menace to society, but in reality society has been a menace to me! I remember back in Miami me and my homeboy psycko had a bitter and deep argument about some dumb shit. He grabbed his stuff and left, and I cried myself to sleep. The next morning I awoke in rage. It was almost as if it had been tattooed on my forehead. My homeboy snipah was living with me at the time. We were really close and always spoke to each other, but today I didn't speak at all. I just looked at him with the expression "leave me alone".

7.

I was full of anger, pain, and resentment. We have to learn how to release our anger in a positive way or it will come out all wrong. I almost shot and killed a girl, and her friend right in front of their kids because I was so full of negative emotions that I didn't know how to cope with. Trust me you could end up doing something that you will regret for the rest of your life by not dealing with your unresolved issues.

8. We tend to lash out on the wrong people when we don't deal with our internal problems. Sometimes I would have mixed emotions after I did something where I went to the extreme. I would feel like it wasn't necessary to do what I did and feel regret. Looking back on those mistakes that I have made makes me take a different approach on how I handle certain situations. I try to think before I react. That day will haunt

9.

me forever, knowing that I could have killed them and their kids! Gang banging turned me into a monster! A few weeks after that incident snipah asked me "blood how were you going to kill everybody with a six shooter"? I told him that I would have went into the pad and reloaded my shit. He laughed and said " you crazy blood". As I think back to the happy moments in my life I ask myself "how did it come to this"? My murderous mind state will not let me rest. Every situation I get into my first thought is " I have to kill you".

MIND PLAYING TRICKS ON ME

10. When I seclude myself I am often asked if I am sick. I think to myself " I am sick, sick in the head that is". I wonder if I am really sick in the head though? Do I have a real serious mental problem? Its complicated, but I believe that I do have a serious mental issue. My mind is playing tricks on me. You would of thought that at the age of twenty I would have figured these tricks out, but I haven't. I believe that I need professional help to deal with my situation. My aunt says I am " a walking time bomb, waiting to explode"! I internalize all my anger, pain, hate, and rage. It is easy to pack it up, but hell unloading it.

THE STRUGGLE

11. I try to be as happy and thankful as possible, but some how my pain always outweighs my joy. Sometimes its psychological, but most of the time it is reality. Even though I am free I still feel trapped. I feel like I have been ripped apart, and now I have to start from scratch. In my weakest state I will still be one of the strongest men that you will ever hear about. Life is a journey that we must embark upon to really and truly understand the meaning of "life". I must continue my journey. Do not be afraid, let me take you into a realm of the unseen.

LETTER TO MY MOM

12. I guess everything is back to normal huh? As soon as you get a little comfortable you feel like it is okay to lay back and relax. All this talk about change, but is it true? Did you fall asleep again? You said " I am holding on", Holding on to what? Nobody can save you but you. You are procrastinating, hoping for a miracle to happen. Unfortunately there are no miracles coming. What are you waiting on? I am not coming back to Miami, not even to visit. This is my good bye letter. See you when I see you. Love juju *was never sent*

LETTER TO MY LITTLE HOMIES

13. What up little funk? What really goes on? Shit I am losing my mind over here. It seems like no matter where I go, or what I do my pain will not cease. I have accepted the fact that my soul won't be able to rest until I am dead. I don't plan on dying though, you all are counting on me and I refuse to let you down. I put up with all the bullshit the world has to offer for you all. My tears won't stop falling, and my heart won't stop aching. I feel paralyzed, tormented, and bruised. Lord knows I try, it seems like trying isn't enough. Do the right thing little funk, don't become like me. Love Jamaal

LOS ANGELES

14. I am currently in Arizona, but I eagerly anticipate going back to Los Angeles. I moved from Miami to L.A. In the beginning of February. I stayed for two weeks and left because my money ran short. Although L.A. Is extremely dangerous, it is both unique and different. L.A. Has shown other countries, states, and cities how to unite. Most people refer to the organizational groups as "gangs", but if you go deeper into the culture you will understand the true purpose of these groups of people. I myself entered one of those groups back in Miami, but this group was not so organized. They had more of a "gang" mentality than a positive and progressive mentality.

15.

After a short period of time the "gang" fell apart. I was left with three homies, the rest were either locked up, snitching, or hiding. It is funny how everyone in a "gang" is suppose to be so tough. A lot of them don't even fight their own battles. I was called upon when money was needed, or work needed to be put in. It was death before dishonor with me. That's how loyal I was. The "gang" didn't hesitate to take advantage of that. Now that I have grown out of that "gang" mentality I consider myself an OG, which stands for original gangster. If anyone needs proof my reputation proves I am authentic.

SECOND LETTER
TO MY MOM

16. Dear mama, I don't mean to be so hard on you. I understand that pushing a person too hard can make them fall instead of move forward. You are my number 1 inspiration. The truest that I know. You stood by my side through the darkest nights, and you were the main reason for my brightest days. We are more like twins instead of mother and son. You have a remedy for making the pain go away every time I ache. You are more than just a mother, your a friend, mentor, inspiration, and all the above. If I don't have you then I don't have nothing. You deserve the whole world, and I am going to get it for you, or die trying.

17. You conceived me and gave me my first breath. So now I live to make you proud with every breath, until my breathing stops. You have officially been certified "best mother ever" Love JuJu

WICKED

18. My thoughts get extremely wicked and deep. I get so deep into my thoughts that they become a realm of evil. I become determined, and anxious to release my demons. I feel like a zombie, like I've let the devil borrow my soul. People often ask me "why are you so mad", or have fear in their eyes. I have wore a face of evil so long that it has consumed me, and we have been made as one. My firm and cold stare shivers souls.

ON THE EDGE

19. One of my most hardest tasks is to stay humble. I am very capable of causing serious injury and damage. I seek and destroy. Muthafuckas think just because I am humble that I am not capable of committing mass amounts of destruction. I realized a long time ago that speaking is ineffective. My actions now replace my words. I am currently working at McDonald's, and the only reason that I haven't choked one of those bitches out yet is because I need the money. I don't need any more bad news spreading around, that's what people want to hear. I promise I'll get through this, and when I do I will make sure they all pay.

SICK OF IT

20. I hate taking bullshit from people, but just today I realized that it is a way of life, especially for blacks. I believe that blacks are now in the most intense and violent state because we are tired of being disrespected day in and day out. As a result of the humiliation and embarrassment we suffer there is extreme violence. We have enough anger, hate, and rage to cause mass amounts of destruction. We have caused so much destruction that it has almost taken away our ability to love each other. I will continue to help my people grow and love, but I won't put up with their bullshit either. You cannot find a solution if you don't recognize the problem.

TRUE

21. When I reflect back to my Miami days it bothers me. I was always serious about whatever I did. When I decided to be a gangster I was in and that was that, no questions or answers needed! I found myself affiliated with individuals who were not serious, and true to what they were into. I found out that it doesn't take long for a fake to break. After that first crack they open up like pussy. We had a gang bang dynasty that crumbled like a cookie in a matter of months because niggaz wasn't true to it. I believe I deserve respect, not for being a gangster, but for being a man, and sticking to what

22. I believe in. I use to believe in everybody else, but now I believe in myself. Why follow when you can lead? I am a natural born leader, but I don't plan on making people take orders. I plan on giving direction to anyone I see falling off track. Leaders have a big amount of responsibility because they are admired and needed so much. There are a lot of leaders that have no intentions on leading you into prosperity. Instead they lead you into traps and misfortunes. If you always hang with individuals who always fail at everything they do, eventually you will become a failure too. I have made up my mind, and there is nothing that anyone can do or say to make me change it! I am a man!

PATIENCE

23. I believe that everyone is blessed, but a lot of us reject our blessings by doing what we want to do instead of doing what we need to do. I have learned that patience really is a virtue. Those who wait appreciate and value their blessings more. You can't always get what you want when you want it. Never say you can't wait because in a lot of cases you have to wait. There is no if, and, or but about that. If eve would have waited for god to return, and asked for permission to eat from that tree she would have not become a fallen angel. Be patient, whatever you desire will eventually come sooner or later.

WAR

24. What is it good for? War has brought loss after loss upon me. When war is the subject we often refer to a physical war. My biggest war is not one to be fought physically but mentally. I am mentally and spiritually at war between my angels and demons. I have come to understand that our physical and mental wars have to be fought through out our whole life. Paradise is a fantasy, happiness comes and goes. My ups and downs helped me understand how serious the war that we are fighting is. We must stop focusing on the physical war and learn how to fight our mental wars.

PUTTING IN WORK

25. When I began putting in work for the set it was intense. It use to make my heart race and adrenaline rush. I use to love rolling deep with my "family", so called family. I felt as though I had nothing to lose, and everything to prove. As I began to get deeper and deeper into the gang lifestyle I started changing, slowly but surely. I started losing touch with reality, and my emotions were invisible sometimes.

26. I have shot at people, killed people, and been shot at. I have learned that these experiences start to take a deep effect on you after while. I noticed myself becoming more solid and lethal. I would zone out sometimes and have to snap back into reality. I have fantasized about being very violent, like beating someone down or killing someone. My aura even changed, I would notice how people would look at me when they seen me. I didn't know that all of these things would happen as a result of my actions.

27. I could hear in my head "kill them, kill them all!".
I started having this passion to kill, I just felt like
I needed to kill someone. It got to the point where
it was like taking drugs, I had became a ridah and
wasn't satisfied if I couldn't ride. I would feel strange
a lot after my experiences, I could just feel death and
danger all around me. I looked at things differently.
Even my movements changed, I was always ready for
action because that was the only way to survive.

28. The first time I was sent on a mission to put in work was unlike the movies, this was surreal. I mean right in front of your face live action. Afterwards when I arrived back on the set I was praised for putting it down and asked how I felt. I didn't feel any different at the moment because it all happened so fast and didn't register, as a matter of fact I didn't feel anything. I couldn't smile, laugh, or cry. This was my introduction to learning how to kill. I was officially down with the set now. I haven't been the same since.

PLAY YOUR PART

29. Those who do not recognize their full potential have limited abilities. You must know your true identity and what you are capable of. My mother and aunt always say "it takes all types to make the world go round" we all have a part to play, and unless you find your position you will be lost. I believe that it is time for us to stop looking up to people and become leaders ourselves. I have much respect for the former black leaders but we must stop dwelling on the past and pick up the pieces. The war has not ended yet, a lot of us may have forgot, or don't want to remember but that doesn't make it disappear.

DETERMINED

30. When I made my decision to move from Miami to Los Angeles it seemed like suicide, considering that I had already been initiated into the bloods. No outsiders allowed is one of the many rules of the hood. Outsiders can easily be infiltrators, cops, or someone that can interfere with business and cause problems in the area. I knew all of this before I made my decision, but I was determined on leaving. My mind was set, there was no turning back. I have come to grips with the fact that I will never really fit in wherever I go, but I will be respected.

WHERE DO I GO FROM HERE?

31. I was not really thinking or caring about becoming a man, but I had the qualities of a man since my childhood. Not being fully prepared for the tasks that men take on can make it extremely hard on a young black man in America. The responsibility of a young black man can make him feel like the world is on his shoulders. We are expected to fall, and born to die young. I feel as though I can't escape no matter where I go or what I do. The average young black man feels like he has no place in the world, because wherever he goes he is not accepted. As a result of this we make the decision to stay in the hood. Where we are sometimes loved, and other times hated.

GOT ME FUCKED UP

32.I understand why so many brothers don't have jobs, and choose to get their money elsewhere. When a brother does get a job its hard to keep. You have to kiss ass and become a pet on a leash just to make some money and accomplish goals. They got me fucked up! If I can't make money, I'll take money. Black man just can't win, its always something. Where the fuck do I go from here? Being black and doing the right thing is hard enough to deal with, among other problems.

INSANE

33. I feel as though the world is my enemy. Everyday that I wake up I am fighting against all odds. How can a man survive and function properly in the world if he has become mentally insane? My confinement is similar to an asylums. By blending in I am able to hide my demons and keep them from reaching the surface. I am seldom in the company of a lot of people, and I don't go out much. I am a very quiet individual, because I know that words are ineffective, at least to me they are. your actions make your words clear and meaningful. Trust me I know.

EERY

34. Me and the homies use to kick it all the time at my pad, but tonight something strange and out of the ordinary would happen. Me and snipah were in the front room kicking it, and psycko was in my room recording his song. After a while of kicking it and watching t.v. Me and snipah fell asleep. I was sleeping on psycko's blow up bed, and snipah was on my fouton. We were only asleep for a couple of hours when all of a sudden snipah woke up screaming real loud. When I heard him screaming I woke up and started screaming. I stopped screaming, looked around, and asked him "what.......... what is it blood!?" Whats wrong? My heart was beating so fast I thought my shit was going

35. To bust out of my chest. Psycko came out of the room looking more scared than us. He said "whats wrong blood", but we were in too much shock to reply. Psycko looked as if he had just seen a ghost. He said "damn blood don't scare me like that". After calming down snipah said "something was touching me blood". I asked him "was it someone you killed"? He said "no" but til this day we don't know what it was. I'll tell you what though, that shit scared the hell out of all of us that night.

HANDLE IT

36. When a problem introduces itself to us we tend to panic, get mad, sad, or frustrated. I believe that problems present opportunity, and whenever opportunity is present we must prove ourselves worthy. So instead of complaining or taking the easy way out we should step up and face it. There will be many tests in life, it is our choice whether we pass or fail. The end is near, and time waits for no one. I am prepared to take on any task that is presented to me. Will you be ready when the time comes?

A REAL MAN

37. A real man recognizes his responsibilities, and takes care of them. A real man faces his problems, and doesn't quit when it seems like he can't win. A real man has respect, discipline, and morals. A real man makes sacrifices and offers help to those in need of assistance. A real man can take care of himself, but is not to proud to accept help when in need. A real man knows his true identity, and does not try to be something he is not. A real man doesn't try to fit in, he is a leader. I wrote this for all the baby boys out there. Its time to grow up my brother, because time waits for no one.

GENOCIDE

38. My brother why do we fight, when we are so much alike? Yet and still we consider each other enemies. Brothers be dying like its a hobby! What are we going to do? Instead of dying and joining our dead brothers we should live for them. I can hear my brothers voices from their graves saying "keep your head up" it seems like we only have one route, straight to the grave! I was more afraid of living than dying, because the responsibility of being a man and pressure of being a gangster weighed heavily on my shoulders. I was eventually driven insane. We must get it together my brothers.

KILLERS

39. It is easy for an individual who has been emotionally murdered to kill. We have been consumed by murder and plagued by death. We have forgotten how to live and learned how to die. Where do we go from here? Some are proud to kill, but I have learned that it only adds more sorrow and pain. I thought I would be embraced because of my loyalty and accepted for being down for whatever. I soon realized that I had fell off the face of the earth because of my actions. Deeper and deeper is where killers dwell. The deeper you get, the worse you feel, the more it haunts you. Lord save us, for we know not what we do. Take a walk in my black chucks with red laces.

TRAUMATIZED

40. I've been traumatized, and the pain has been embedded in me. There is no turning back, this is eternal. Everyday I learn a new lesson, I feel that it is necessary for a ghetto bird to learn how to fly. They say if you cry you are a punk. I think I cry more than a lot of other men, and I am far from being a punk. As a matter of fact I am one of the hardest brothers that you will ever hear about. How can an individual deal with their pain without doing drugs, drinking alcohol, or smoking cigarettes? The only reason I am here is because of god's grace and mercy. I should have been dead a long time ago.

DR JEKYLL & MR HIDE

41. One minute I am crying my heart out, and the next I am ready to terrorize the world. To all those that don't understand stay the fuck out of my way! This is my life and I am going to live it how I want to. Life is so serious that it is hard to smile. The world is tearing me down. Lord save me, these times are critical. Kill now, cry later

NO SURRENDER

42. No retreat, no surrender, death before dishonor. Though I walk through the valley of hell I shall fear no man, demon, nor devil. I will not surrender in the presence of danger. We must fall in order to rise. When I fall I don't stay down and accept defeat, I rise! I believe I can achieve anything that I set out to accomplish. We must love and believe in ourselves, and stop letting other people control our lives. In order to free yourself you must be yourself. No retreat, no surrender. Don't give up.

SHADY

43. What you think could be a dream come true could really be your worse nightmare. A lot of people and things that seemed real actually turned out to be fake. It has gotten so scandalous that I don't know who to trust, but I have learned to trust god above all because he is the only one that can save us. There is so much evil going around that its hard to do good. Even though there is so much evil spreading like germs, I will continue on correcting things instead of making more mistakes.

EVIL

44. Evil is no longer visible because we have been consumed by it. What was once wrong and rejected now has been accepted. Morals have been abandoned and deserted, the wickedness has overpowered us. Evil requires no contemplation or forethought, only action can satisfy the thought of evil. We tend to lose focus in the presence of evil, not recognizing that evil is present. We must keep our eyes open, meaning keep an open mind and be aware of the evil that constantly stalks us like our own shadow. Evil is alive and on the prowl, so be aware.

JUDGEMENTS

45. Don't judge a book by its cover. Many of us (including myself) tend to prejudge individuals to satisfy our curiosity. To underestimate someone's abilities is a big mistake that we often make. What humans mostly overlook is the fact that the mind is deadlier and more efficient than physical strength. By using our brains we eliminate the hassle and frustration of having to use our physical strength. A lot of tasks that seem difficult to us are actually simple. All you have to do is put your mind to it and do it. Have courage and stand up for what you believe in.

5 MINUTES AWAY

46. 5 minutes away from death row is where I found myself as I stood in the middle of the street. One night me and the homies were kicking it doing the usual, smoking weed and drinking old English. We were in the back alley of my apartment building slipping and off guard. As we made our way back to my apartment we laughed and joked, not knowing what would take place later on that night. Once we were in the pad we kicked it a little while longer and drifted off to sleep. We were so faded and the air conditioner was so loud and cold that it would of have taken a bomb to wake us up. We were robbed

47. in our sleep. They could have murdered us in our sleep but didn't. I was awaken by the sound of my mothers voice. She was screaming my name to see if I was still alive. Her screams made me jump out of my sleep. I woke up the homies while searching for our guns. When they woke up we realized that we got jacked. As I headed to the front door to let my mother know that we were alright I noticed that my screen was pulled off, my window was up, and my front door was spray painted. On my front door was a pitch fork with the numbers 7 and 4 in the middle of it.

48. 7 and 4 meant GD, which stood for gangster disciple. It was necessary to have all other gangs information. After calming down and getting our emotions together we thought about our situation long and hard. All of our minds were saying "who could have done this"? We came to several conclusions but none of them were correct. We were puzzled by this event that took place. Our confusion caused us to lock in on the wrong target. My suspicions grew more and more until there was no more evidence needed.

49. I almost ended up killing the wrong person. This is a perfect example to think before you react. A lot of people get to the point where they don't care who gets it, and that's not right. What if you killed someone and found out that person had nothing to do with what happened to you? Me personally I would feel bad, like damn it didn't have to go down like that. I was going to blow this guy's heart out his chest but his aunt walked up. 5 minutes later the police rolled by.

DEATH AROUND THE CORNER

50. When I began gang banging I never really thought about my own death. As I got deeper into the lifestyle thoughts of my own death and visions of my slain corpse began haunting me. I started having nightmares about getting killed, and even though I was in a dream state it seemed real. I cried a lot thinking about how much hurt and pain my death would bring upon my love ones. Death is spreading so fast, and it has gotten so contagious that it makes me wonder "why am I so special, why haven't I died yet".

DEEP

51. How deep can one go without becoming trapped? My memories faded as my wickedness enhanced. If happiness was the surface of life I would be at rock bottom. Pain has moved into my heart and made it its home. My mind travels at the speed of a lightning bolt. I often get caught up in my own thoughts, entrenched in evil and driven by hate. I am a fallen angel that has been consumed by the ways of the wicked. Label me whatever you want, I am all the above! Take a journey into the mind of a madman, and pray that you make it back safe.

MUCH MORE TO OFFER

52. To all my brothers and sisters, old and young, the world has much more to offer than guns, drugs, and death. These devils have kept us brainwashed far too long. The problem is that we are not informed, and encouraged to take advantage of opportunities when they appear. We must expand our minds to greater levels of thinking. The only way to reach higher levels is to learn. Learn as much as you can, but remember to take it one day at a time. Take chances, make mistakes, and learn from them. The world is on our shoulders, sometimes we fall but don't stay down.

STAND ALONE

53. I believe if you can stand alone you are capable of leading a nation. We need to stop worrying about what other people say and stand up for what we believe in. I didn't and still don't care about how others feel or think about me, because I am going to do what I want to do. I accept advice and encouragement, but I am still going to do what I feel is the right thing to do. Nobody can stop me, I am eternal!

JUST DON'T KNOW

54. In the battle field is where I roam, traumatized from the war that I have been fighting my whole life. When I close my eyes my pain becomes more clear. My every move is cautious, that's how serious life is to me. I wish I could go to sleep and wake up in heaven. I wouldn't feel anymore pain or grief, only peace. They just don't know what it takes to walk in my chucks.

PRECIOUS

55. The most precious thing in life is life itself. To be able to watch a baby be born and grow is beautiful. Their eyes shine like stars, and their faces reveal their innocence. Their touch is soft enough to make a cold hearted killer feel warm inside. Their first words and first steps are like watching a miracle take place. Babies are the future, if we mistreat them, harm them, and kill them, there will not be a future. There shouldn't be any abortions. If you can have sex and make a baby, then you should be able to take care of it.

BECAUSE OF YOU (GOD)

56. It is because of you that I am still alive. It is because of you that I can function after being driven insane. It is because of you that my hope gets restored after being broken. Your unconditional love gives me the strength to carry on. You have lifted the curtain off my soul, and let your light shine down on it. Yet again you have saved me from the wickedness of this world. Please lord forgive me for my sins, in my heart I truly desire to do what is right. You have my unconditional love. Yours truly shadow

FUCK AMERIKKKA!!!!!

57. You just don't know who you are fucking with! You have destroyed the lives of many brothers and sisters. You have robbed us of our hope, education, history, belongings, and identity. We have pleaded for your help, but all you did was spit in our face. We were enslaved and beaten because of the color of our skin. You have poisoned us with guns and drugs. My people feel worthless, and it is all because of you. What are we suppose to do? How are we suppose to feel? You have ignored our pain for years! It is clear now but you still can't see!

LIFE & DEATH

58. I have come up with a theory that can explain the reason for life and death. I heard through the grapevine that whenever someone dies a baby is born. I figure a life must be sacrificed in order for a new one to be created. Life equals death, and death equals life. I believe an incomplete life will cause death, and in turn give the newly created life a chance to live and serve its purpose. I cannot say that my theory is fully accurate, but it is in some way correct. We must live to die, and die to live.

SOPHISTICATED

59. I am perceived as one of low intelligence because of my image. I have become deeply rooted and educated. I am misunderstood by simple minded people. Most of the judgments made about me are inaccurate. Often by myself because my views of the world and its inhabitants differ from those who are not open minded and in tune with the universe. Aggressive, humble, and meticulous are three words to describe me. My visions are clear, but they tend to become blurry at times. If your mind isn't deep enough don't try and understand me.

THE DARKSIDE

60. Withdrawn from the light, dwelling beneath the surface, consumed by wickedness. No where to run, no where to hide, once you are in you can't escape from the dark side. My heart feels frozen, and my eyes are stiff. The dark side has altered my thinking and way of living. I have evolved from the victim to the predator. No longer gasping for air because I have adapted to the dark side. ETERNAL!

MUCH LOVE

61. My grandpa frank and grandma Thelma have shown me the greatest level of love that a man can get. They have sacrificed their own privacy by making their home my home. They have taught me valuable lessons about life, and have granted me access to the other side of the world. My programmed thought was to rebel against it, but through a brief process I have chosen to embrace their teachings. My grandpa and grandma have shown me how to look past defaults and errors and find the good. They have put their hearts and souls on the line. They deserve much love.

HARD

62. What is hard on the outside can be fragile on the inside. When it comes to humans we remain strong on the outside so no one can reach our fragile inside. We are not comfortable being weak so we hide our vulnerability. Our masks and costumes disguise us. We hide behind shields and barriers to keep from being hurt. Who in their right mind wants to be hurt? The funny thing about this is we end up getting hurt anyway. A lot of us don't know how to deal with pain, so we try to block it out and avoid it.

LETHAL

63. My gangster mentality has programmed me. The knowledge and wisdom that has been installed in me along with my battlefield tactics have molded me into a lethal weapon. I am not a ordinary "thug" as they like to call us. I am far greater than most think. Most believe that they are greater than the next because of their possessions. I dwell in a spiritual realm where material things don't exist. They may seem real, but its just a delusion. All the money in the world cannot buy me. I cannot be bought or sold, because I am eternal!

PHENOMENON

64. Through all the dirt and darkness that I have been through I can still come out and shine! That is phenomenal, incredible, amazing, and all the above. I owe it all to god. Without you there would be no me. Thank you from the depths of my soul, I appreciate everything that you have done for me. I hope that my life and everything that I have been through can inspire others who are struggling to find their way. Seeing others succeed will really make me feel successful. I would be honored to be apart of their success.

HOPELESS

65. Tired of living, tired of trying, tired of feeling sorrow. I feel like I am going in circles. No matter how far I go I always end up at a dead end street. Show me a sign that everything will be okay lord. My pain has overwhelmed me, I feel hopeless. What is there to look forward to? Positivity has disappeared. My hopes have been shattered yet again.

AGAINST THE GRAIN

66. All my life I have went against the grain. I have been accepted, but I never really fit in. I am currently living in the suburbs, and once again I don't fit in. I gave up on fitting in a long time ago. I just don't give a fuck! You can love me or hate me, it doesn't matter. I know my true identity and what I am capable of. What everyone else thinks is not important. Fuck the world! With a big dick!

WHAT LIES AHEAD

67. There is no possible way that you can prepare yourself for everything that lies ahead. There are obstacles that are visible and invisible. We are more vulnerable to the invisible obstacles because we don't know exactly when they will appear. We must walk on faith and not by sight. Beware of what lies ahead.

HAUNTED

68. The presence of something or someone that is not visible haunts me. Today I was laying on my stomach in my bed, when I closed my eyes I could feel the presence of something or someone standing over me. There is never anyone there when I open my eyes. In some of my dreams I have had to fight to wake up because there was something holding me down trying to kill me. When I wake up sweating there is nothing there.

FACES OF DEATH

69. Have you ever seen the expression on someones face right before they die? Me and my homies use to play around with guns all the time. We would point them at each other as if we were playing Russian roulette. One night I took the bullets out of the chambers of my 357. my homies didn't know that I had taken the bullets out because they were in the living room. I came out of my room, walked up to my homie psycko, pointed the gun at his head and pulled the trigger. The gun clicked and everything seemed to pause. The expression that he revealed was death.

BLOODS

70. What lead me to gang banging was my lack of direction and love. I didn't have anyone to show me how to be a man. I joined the bloods because I thought that they were similar to the black panthers. I believed that the bloods could lead me into the right direction. Bloods have dignity, love, respect, and courage. Through a brief process I found out that all bloods are not the same. That's life though, can't have the good without the bad. To all the true bloods that died for the cause, and all the homies that are still alive you have my unconditional love! I represent to the fullest! PIRU LOVE

SACRIFICES

71. I have learned that sacrifices must be made in order to achieve what you desire. My process of becoming a man has shown me that I cannot always do what I want to do, but I am obligated to do what I need to do. A lot of individuals in the world are so caught up in doing what they want to do that they forget about doing what they need to do. Its just the opposite for those who take care of their needs and not their wants. Life is all about balance. Everything must be equal in order to maintain and prosper.

IN GOD'S HANDS

72. I have done all I can do now, now is the time to put all of my problems in god's hands. Suicide seems like the best way to get free at this point. Only god can help me now. I must carry on and be strong for the dead homies and all my love ones. I have carried the weight of the world on my shoulders all my life, so obstacles are nothing new to me. I am a souljah! There is nothing that can stop me from getting where I am going.

CHOSEN

73. I believe I am one of the chosen few. Not because I am better than everyone else, but because I have survived and overcame obstacles that I didn't believe I could overcome. When I felt like I had no more will power left somehow I always found a way to get up and keep pushing. My purpose was unknown, so I felt like I didn't have a reason to live, or care. I have hoped and wished that I could die. I have been face to face with death, and for some reason I am still alive.

FAITH

74. I have learned to walk on faith and not by sight. Although I walk on faith and put my trust in god I still make plans. My faith in god is strong. There has been many times that I lost my faith and forgot the lord was and always will be with me. Every time I lose my faith and regain it my confidence in the lord and myself becomes ten times stronger. The lord will test our faith by putting obstacles in front of us. Our choices determine if we pass or fail.

READY FOR WHATEVER

75. I have learned that tomorrow will always be different than today and yesterday. With each new day we must hope for the best and prepare for the worse. Experience has shown me that you can have the best day of your life today, and the worse day of your life tomorrow. I have learned to adapt to whatever the next day will bring. This technique might sound simple, but it is not easy to do. Especially if you have never been put in a position where you have to adapt. Flexibility is the key to survival in all aspects.

EASY WAY OUT

76. Living is far greater than dying to me. Dying is easy compared to the tasks and responsibilities that life requires to be fulfilled in order to live. Adults have the highest level of responsibility because they are the providers. The pressure weighs so heavy on me that sometimes I go to sleep hoping that I won't wake up. The thought of waking up to another day is more painful than dying.

Can't fade this

77. To all the muthafuckas who tried and keep trying to fade my strength, wisdom, courage, and motivation, let it be known that souljahs don't fold. You coward ass muthafuckas will never be able to break my spirit. After all that I have been through I am still stomping in my red chucks. Only true souljahs kick up dust until the wheels fall off. I am rolling solo and still holding it down. I am broke as a muthafuckin joke still walking with my chest poked out and head held high. Fuck the world!

BETTER DAYS

78. Through all the pain and hardships that we endure in life, we still must continue to live on and search for better days. Sometimes happiness seems so distant that I stop reaching for it and just let my sorrow drown me. I have come to understand that life is a mixture of good and bad. Sometimes things get really bad, and sometimes things are really good. You never know what may happen throughout your day, but as long as you live to see the next day there is a possibility that it may be a good day. Keep your head up.

ALWAYS SOMETHING

79. Every time I make it through one door I get another one slammed in my face. Lord knows I am trying to do whats right. After getting so many doors slammed in my face I tend to give up. I start questioning my intentions, "what am I trying for, do I really care". A young black man's confidence gets beaten down so often that he eventually loses it. I am trying to live a steady day by day life, but in the process I become entangled in problems that appear out of no where.

RAGE WITHIN

80. The rage within me has developed out of my unbearable pain. After the pain has done its damage, and finally settles, that's when the rage emerges. Sometimes I find myself attacking or being defensive to people who haven't done anything to me. My rage is to the point that I refuse to let anyone do anything wrong to me without retaliating. I have evolved from the prey to the predator. I have learned that being a souljah means knowing when to attack. I am trying to learn how to control my rage.

HOLDING ON

81. Even though I feel so close to the edge, I am still holding on hoping that I don't fall. Its a miracle that I haven't committed suicide. As my tears drain my spirit I fall to my knees and thank god for everything he has done for me. Whenever I feel like I can't go on anymore the lord thrusts me back in motion. When your strength is at its weakest point and your heart has almost stopped beating, who will you call upon? God will be with me every step of the way on my journey.

PROBLEMS

82. My problems are similar to pests, when I get rid of one three more appear. They come so often that I don't get a chance to breathe. I am being mentally beaten to death. I feel like putting on a straight jacket and calling it quits. I have no pity for myself because pity is for the weak. My problems will not go away unless I face them, so I don't have a choice. There are no breaks, or rest for the weary.

OBSERVE

83. One of my abilities that enables me to see the picture clearly is how I observe. I watch movements, actions, my surroundings, and the people around me. I like to study people, and how they operate. I try to be aware of what is going on. Many individuals refuse to see whats real because being naive has trapped them. Being naive is just the same as being a fool to me. We must open our minds to all levels of thinking. I keep an open mind, so I am subjected to learning as much as possible.

NEVER BE THE SAME

84. I never knew a person could feel so somber until now. I have felt pain before, but this is deeper than anything I have ever imagined. My sorrow and tears have drowned me. I know now that this will stick with me for the rest of my life. I have changed so much that it is impossible to go back to how it used to be. Reflecting back to my childhood brightens the darkness that constantly surrounds me. I feel like I have crossed a bridged that collapsed when I got to the other side.

CAN'T STOP WON'T STOP

85. I give respect to anyone who deserves it. When my respect is lost it is hard to regain. It is a known fact that I get down for mine, but those who do not know me feel as though they can disrespect without suffering the consequences. Time and time again I must show these disrespectful, no courage having, loud mouth busters that I am not the one they wanna fuck with. I try to avoid using violence, but in some cases it is necessary. I can't stop, and won't stop putting you punk muthafuckas in check.

IS IT WRONG?

86. From what I understand there is nothing wrong with being strong. A lot of people try to make me feel like it is wrong to be strong. If I was weak everyone would take advantage of me, but because I am so strong they can't, and that's the problem. It seems like everyone is mad at me because they can't be as strong as me. Its funny how someone can be jealous of you and pretend like they are your friend to get what you have.

BREAKING ME DOWN

87. The enormous amount of hate that has formed deep in my heart is breaking me down. I need as much love as I can get. Fake love will only introduce more hate to the black hole deep in my heart. I believe only real love can heal my sickness. I have lost my mind. I feel like I am spiraling out of control! There are too many thoughts running through my mind that I cannot control. I am mentally unstable at this point.

WORLD ON MY SHOULDERS

88. I've got a thousand problems surrounding me, but what makes my circumstances even harder is trying to hold my head up high and stay strong even though the world is on my shoulders. The pressure is weighing heavily on me at this point. I have come so far that giving up would be suicide. In a worldly view it would be impossible to carry the world on my shoulders. I have learned that anything is possible as long as you believe.

BENEATH THE SURFACE

89. The commonly known word "truth" is often misrepresented and misused. I believe the truth is hidden beneath the surface, while lies disguise themselves and are perceived as the truth. As time races forward revelations reveal that the corruption of the world will continue to grow and spread. We must open our eyes so we can see what is taking place. We are living a lie, and everything we think we understand we really don't have a clue about. The truth is beneath the surface. Don't die living a lie.

BETTER OFF DEAD

90. My pain and suffering causes me to feel like I am better off dead. My circumstances are so bad that I feel hopeless. How did it come to this? My heart has more hate than love, and I see more destruction than rebuilding. I am looked upon as if I am evil, when I truly have good intentions. Things never change no matter how hard I try. I just don't give a shit anymore. My destiny is to die young, and I am ready.

IN TIME

91. Even though my future seems hopeless I am still praying for better days. I know in my heart that everything I dream of will come true in time. As long as I have faith in god and myself I believe that I will make it. Each new day brings a new obstacle. I will not let these obstacles keep me down. In time the world shall be mine! Get ready

SILENT

92. I am mostly silent because I speak through my thoughts, being silent helps me observe the picture clearly. My judgments and understanding of whatever I focus on become more accurate. The ability to learn is one of the most efficient abilities that we humans have. I believe that if I am constantly speaking I am cutting my learning process short. I also stay silent to avoid conflicts and debates. Sometimes it feels like I am invisible. I am also silent because many of the topics that are discussed don't interest me.

COURAGE

93. My positivity seems like it rides a roller coaster. When I start feeling like there is nothing here for me, and I don't have anything to live for, my courage keeps the flesh of my broken spirit active. When my faith has disappeared, and my expectations run low I began to feel hopeless. As my negative thoughts marinate in my mind I begin sinking into a sea of depression. My courage is linked to my survival, and helps me move forward when I feel stuck.

DESTINY

94. What does life mean to a person surrounded by death? Death has been so close to me that I stopped being afraid of it and began to embrace it. All the deaths that I have witnessed make me feel like it is my destiny to die young. Even though the odds are always against me, deep in my heart I know that this is not my destiny. I know that my purpose consists of much more than gang banging. I want to live life to its fullest extent, after that I can die and rest in peace.

TIL THE DEATH OF ME

95. I will fight to instill hope into those who feel hopeless. I will fight to live for all my brothers and sisters who have died searching for a better way to live. I aspire to achieve every goal that I set out to achieve. I will fight to prosper in a world where I am expected to fall. I will fight to inspire and educate young black men and women. I will fight to build optimism and self esteem in the black youth. I will continue to fight for my people until the death of me.

ROLLER COASTER

96. So many ups and downs make me feel like I am riding a roller coaster. There is only so much I can take without becoming sick. Life is a gamble and we never know what to expect. Each day is different than the former one. I am tired of riding this roller coaster. I want to get off and get the fuck on with my life. I am not stable, and haven't been since birth. Some shit always took place that altered my fate and destiny. Now I am just riding this wave not knowing where I may end up.

GIVE BACK

97. I believe that god has given me strength to persevere so that I can be a reflection of hope and inspiration. I have been given strength and love to be used as a tool to overcome my every day struggles. In turn I must contribute my inheritance to another who is in need of assistance. I understand that I am not the only one in a deep and intense struggle. I must pass my strength and knowledge on to some one who is facing some of the same things that I have faced or worse.

LIFE IS

98. Life is a mystery, life is an adventure, life Is a journey. Life is precious, life is beautiful, life is exciting. Life can be terrible at times but there is no good without the bad. From now until my demise I will capture and treasure every moment of happiness and joy, so when I look back on my life it won't consist of tears and sorrow. Life is too precious to only recognize the bad that happens to us without recognizing the good.

OUTCAST

99. I feel like society has rejected me and forced me to live as an outcast. I believe that the real "American way" is to strong arm anyone and everyone to get what they want. Truthfully its robbery! Living in America I have witnessed people act or dress and even talk a certain way to be accepted. Those who refuse to comply with these rules and regulations will become outcasts, separated, and ignored. I see no love in this so called "American way". All I see is a bunch of selfish, money hungry fools that will push aside anyone to get what they want.

DREAMS

100. In a lot of ways our dreams warn and help us predict and see the future. I believe god sends us messages through our dreams, and in many other ways. A lot of us ignore the signs he tries to show us because our flesh weakens and blinds us. I believe that the dreams we can remember are significant and the ones we cannot remember are meaningless. Pay attention to your dreams.

ALONE

101. Sometimes I feel like I am all alone in this crazy, mischief world. I know for a fact that I am far from selfish, so it can't be my mind playing tricks on me. I rarely get lonely and company is not an issue. I am a very charismatic person and can easily attract people. Most of the time I am by myself just thinking about all types of things. If I ever get married I hope this doesn't affect my relationship with my wife (but I know it will).

DON'T UNDERSTAND

102. I hate when people criticize what they are afraid of and do not understand. I hate the selfishness that the people of this world carry in their hearts. Being a human means that we aren't suppose to know and never will understand everything that goes on and happens in this world, and the universe. Even Albert Einstein didn't have an answer for every question. There isn't enough research in the world that can help you understand everything.

SINCERE

103. A lot of men can't handle being in the company of a beautiful woman without engaging in sexual activities, or being able to control their sexual desires. There is nothing wrong with being attracted to a woman, but if you are going to try to have sex with every woman you find attractive you are going to have a big problem! Being in the company of a woman is satisfying to me. A lot of women talk to me and like me because I am sincere and honest. I don't have any gimmicks or tricks up my sleeve.

PUSH

104. Whenever something good happens to me something bad happens right after it. It seems like a distraction that occurs whenever I get through an obstacle. The outcome is both positive and negative, because although it angers me it adds fuel to my flame, and drives me to strive even harder. I have learned to convert negative into positive. My obstacles cannot stop me, they only make me push harder.

IT HAS BEGUN

105. My rise to the top is now in full effect! As god is my witness I cannot be stopped. I thought my journey was over and done with, but it has just begun. I will slowly rise one day at a time, thanks to god. I see and feel change and opportunity arising, and I feel encouraged, enlightened, joyful and appreciative. This is why we should never give up, because you never know what opportunities will arise that can help you get closer to achieving what you desire.

THANK GOD

106. Thank god for the pleasure and the pain, sun shine and rain. Thank god for life. Thank god for all the opportunities that he has blessed me to see. Thank god for having my back and showing me unconditional love even when I am wrong. Thank god for keeping me covered. Watch my back father you are the only one I can trust. Take me to heaven when I die, and let my soul rest in peace.

AGAINST ALL ODDS

107. It seems like every time I get ahead there is always something or someone that is constantly trying to pull me back. I feel like its me against the world. Through my eyes it looks like I don't stand a chance. My mind says "just give up, you can't win", but my heart says "you are too strong to give up, and you have came too far to stop now. I am going to prove to the whole world that I am worthy.

UNCERTAIN

108. Only god knows what the future holds for me. All I can do is pray and stay strong. I feel very uncomfortable not having control of my life, and not knowing exactly where I will end up or what will happen next. I feel lost a lot, I don't fit in and am misunderstood. I have been trying to find out what is best for me, but can't seem to hit the nail on the head. Life without purpose is meaningless. I hope I find out what my purpose is, so I don't have to stay stuck and confused.

ANOTHER DAY

109. Another day goes by while I sit back feeling institutionalized, uncertain of my future. Although I cannot predict the future I still hope and pray for better days. I tend to get discouraged waiting for things to get better, and the more I try to better my situation the worse it gets. So I just end up stuck. I feel trapped! I keep looking for something, anything to give me some hope, but I find nothing. My life Is meaningless.

SUICIDAL VISIONS

110. For the past few days I have been seeing images of me killing myself. I've seen myself cutting my wrist, and I have been hearing my mind tell me "just do it". One day me and my grandpa were riding pass a lake and something said "all you have to do is jump in and drown, all your pain will go away". I pictured myself drowning and looked away from the lake.

SEXAHOLIC

111. I can't lie I absolutely love sex! I have an enormous amount of passion when it comes to having sex. I love women and everything about them. A woman with pretty feet turns me on the most. My attraction is strong, almost magnetic. I am a freak, but to a certain extent. All that kinky shit like licking feet, licking assholes, and all that other crazy shit I don't do. My passion and desire is what sets me aside from a lot of people.

ZOMBIE

112. There are times when I feel like my soul has been removed, and all I have left is my flesh. It makes me feel like a brain dead walking corpse. If you take a good look at society you will see that the world is full of zombies. We are a bunch of lost souls seeking pleasure, but never get enough. Our pleasure temporarily satisfies us and makes us forget how empty and unfulfilled we are. We feed off of each others misery, and breed generations of cannibals that devour each other. We continue to satisfy our appetite for destruction, instead of being filled with knowledge.

MY LIFE

113. My life is significant and intriguing yet tragic. To only be twenty years old and experience what I have been through is enough to drive a sane individual insane. Sometimes I feel like I belong in a straight jacket, because I am a threat to society and myself. I have had some very joyful moments in my life, but I have had some very somber moments too. I believe that life should be appreciated and not taken advantage of. I have an enormous amount of pain dwelling within me. Its so deep that I don't have a broken bone in my body, but yet and still I feel cripple.

PROMISE

114. I promise to god that if he helps me cross this bridge in my life I won't go back. I have been held back for too long. Now is the time for me to break free from these invisible chains that have stopped me from prospering. I am putting all my faith in you lord, thanks for everything you have done for me. Yours truly shadow

ALWAYS ON TIME

115. I know for a fact that god doesn't do things when we want him to, but he is always on time. Every time I feel myself slipping god is always there to help me get back on track. God is my savior, when there is no where else to go, and no one else I can depend on, I can depend on god. He has never let me down, he always made a way out of no way. Put your trust and faith in god, he will be there for you when no one else is. Trust me I know

VIOLENT

116. I believe the most violent individuals were once victims. The pain, suffering, humiliation, and frustration inflicts so much damage that it causes them to become extremely violent. Some are able to channel their anger and use it to their advantage, but a lot have problems controlling their anger. The most violent individuals are the ones that have the most painful pasts. Many of us use violence to conceal the pain we feel. Some become suicidal instead of violent. If you look beyond what is visible you will understand.

STRAIGHT SOULJAH

117. First of all I want to say rest in peace to Larry Davis and send my condolences to his family. Being a souljah to me means you will fight when no one else will. You will stand up when everyone else backs down, and you will speak when everyone else is speechless. A souljah is a person who will go against all odds and overcome. In order to be a souljah you must accept the fact that there will be times when you are all alone. A souljah cannot always follow, he or she must be able to lead just as well. I am a souljah, there is no doubt about that. *dedicated to snipah*

IMPOSSIBLE

118. Impossible means something that cannot be done. By me being born black the odds were already against me. Many of us feel lost, confused, and hopeless. We often self destruct because there is no possibility of life In the future. I have learned that god can make the impossible possible, as long as you have faith. As long as you have faith in god and yourself anything is possible!

WHO AM I

119. In order to love yourself you must know yourself. Take a look in the mirror and ask yourself who am I? Examine yourself, study yourself, know your strengths and weaknesses. Get to know you. We spend so much time trying to figure other people out that we forget about ourselves. Take care of you first. I am not saying be selfish, I am saying you should be important to you. When we start taking care of ourselves and loving ourselves we won't have to wait for someone else to come along and do it for us.

INVISIBLE

120. I believe that black people are ignored so much that we become invisible to society. Whenever we do get some attention it is for something horrendous and depicts us as monsters, while whites get credit for heroic acts. The only blacks that are recognized are the ones with power and money. The sell outs and busters. People like to tell you to do the right thing, but we seldom get rewarded or acknowledged for doing the right thing. That's why so many blacks don't give a shit, and do what they want to do.

USE YOUR BRAIN

121. A mind is a terrible thing to waste! Nothing in this world is more powerful than the human brain. It is a shame that we would rather use man made things instead of using our god given abilities. This is not the wizard of oz, nobody is going to give you a muthafuckin brain! You have to use the one you have, and use it wisely. A lot of what happens in our lives is psychological, its in your head, that is where the battlefield is! If you can win there, you can win in reality.

CAN'T HIDE IT

122. No matter how much I try to hide my demons they always find a way to reach the surface. Deep in my soul lies an ongoing battle between the good in me and the evil in me. I often hide my pain behind a wall of solid confidence and strength. What is strange about me is the high capacity that I have to do good and evil. I can be the most humorous, joyful, respectful, and intelligent individual you can come across, but I can also be a dangerous, homicidal, arrogant, psychopath! My split personality is what tears me up internally.

THE ESSENCE

123. The essence of life and every aspect of it has been lost and forgotten. Traditions and cultures have been tarnished and tampered with. I look at society and feel disgusted by what I see. The people of this world have become selfish, greedy, disrespectful, and unrealistic. Our values and morals have faded away. We have become plagued by materials. A lot of people are full of shit. To be straight up this world and everything in it has become watered down.

SUCCESS

124. Once I cross this bridge of failure and reach success I am going to triumph and celebrate like Jesus has returned! I want to see how many smiles, frowns, and mean mugs I receive as a result of my success. To me success doesn't mean becoming famous, or attaining superstar status. Success to me means achieving a feeling of completion. I know for a fact that my soul will never have peace unless I fulfill my destiny and reach that level of completion that I desire.

MAKING HISTORY

125. Damn, today is the day we make history and I didn't even get a chance to vote. Even though I know that one individual cannot change the world by themselves, I still hope that Obama wins. I already know that if he wins he will become an automatic target for assassination. That's just how the system is set up. A black man with knowledge and power can change things, and this world doesn't want change.

PARALLEL MINDS

126. It is amazing how you can meet a person, get to know them, and feel like you have known them your whole life. I met the homie joey at the Fam bam studio where I am recording my album "it has begun". From the beginning we had a connection but didn't really notice it until we began to get into a deep, intellectual conversation while working on one of my songs. I believe it shocked both of us when we seen how much we were alike. We talked for hours about different subjects. I was amazed at how similar our views were.

WHAT WOMEN WANT

127. From what I understand women want to feel loved. They yearn for attention, and lust for intimacy and romance. Women want someone who is intellectual, someone that can understand them. A woman wants someone they can talk to, someone that can listen as well as they give advice. Women are extra sensitive, so you must be extra careful how you treat a woman. I love everything about women, as a man I feel like they complete us.

ALL WRONG

128. Today was terrible, for some reason everything just went completely wrong. My mind couldn't handle the pressure, I began to lose my patience. In the spur of the moment I fell astray. Too many things were happening at once, and I just couldn't take that shit so I snapped, which made things even worse! My attitude was "fuck it". When you see things going wrong and there is nothing you can do about it that's how you feel.

A FOOL

129. I would be a fool to go out and get a woman that I am unable to take care of, or even assist for that matter. The circumstances that I am currently in won't even allow me to take care of myself. Why bother trying to get into a relationship knowing that my circumstances won't allow me to comply with the rules and regulations that relationships require. I would like to be In a loving relationship, but I feel like right now is not the right time. Maybe later on down the line I will get that opportunity.

GOOD AND BAD

130. I hope that when my life is over and my destiny has been fulfilled, people will be able to see that I am human too. I want my life to be captured from beginning to end, so it is clear that I was an angel plagued and tormented by demons. Let my life be an example that there is hope for the future. I believe that even the worse, demonic, cold hearted individuals have a little good in them.

RESTLESS

131. I believe that there are souls trapped on this earth that cannot rest, because they have either died violently, or died without fulfilling their purpose. These are the so called "ghosts" that we see from time to time. Throughout my whole life from the beginning to the present my soul has been at war. Whenever I die I hope that my soul will finally have a chance to rest in peace.

DIE TOGETHER

132. One night a young man was murdered in the parking lot of a club directly across the street from the back of my apartment building. I was asleep in my room at the time that the murder took place. I didn't hear anything that night, but I can remember my heart beating real fast, and my chest rising like my soul was coming out of my body. As my heart began to beat faster and faster it felt like I was dying. After my chest sunk back into position and my heart slowed down to its normal pace it was like nothing ever happened. Can you believe I was asleep during that whole ordeal. The next

133. Day I found out that the young brother who was murdered got gunned down over a woman that he punched in the face because his girl got into a fight with her over some money. I felt him die.

REACH FOR THE SKY

134. The sky is the limit, and anyone can have whatever they want if their desire is strong enough. It disappoints me when I see people settle for less, instead of obtaining what they desire to have. I believe that we as a people, and as individuals should try to get a grip on what we cannot grasp, instead of holding on to what we already have. I don't want anyone to miss my concept. Greed causes self destruction. All I want is to inspire people to reach higher.

DISTANT

135. I have grown more distant than ever to society, my family, and associates because of my experiences and the effect that they have had on me. I see things differently and act differently. I am withdrawn a lot. I don't go out much and don't hang around a lot of people. I actually like solitude, it helps me get a piece of mind. I don't want anyone to feel like I don't like them or think that I am better than them. I just like being alone a lot.

BEYOND AND ABOVE

136. My whole outlook on life goes beyond and above many individuals perceptions. Life is precious and beautiful when you get through the dark and gloomy side effects. I hate to be pessimistic because it makes my spirit, hope, and optimism disappear. I believe that god wants me to go beyond and above, instead of behind and below. My purpose is even greater than I can imagine! I just don't understand it right now, that is why I am having such a difficult time. Hopefully time will reveal my purpose.

OUTRAGEOUS

137. When I was a lot younger I came up with this theory that all of the older women would be old and used up by the time I reached manhood. It was an outrageous theory, but it shows how strong the curiosity of a child's mind is. I had to be between the ages of 5 and 10 at the time. One afternoon I was watching television and got caught in awe by the beauty of these older women. I wished that I was older so I could have one of them. All of a sudden I started crying! I thought to myself "I'll never get a woman that beautiful, because when I reach their age they will be old and wrinkled.

THE GHETTO

138. A place where evil dwells in the minds of the old and young. Where caged souls, cry, beg, and plead to be set free. A place where lost souls roam searching for some type of inner peace. It is very hard to live in the ghetto and not succumb to the pessimistic and self destructive ways that evolve from unbearable circumstances. The government doesn't care about the people who live there, and a lot of people who live there don't care about themselves, or anything for that matter. There has to be a heaven, because living in the ghetto is like living in hell.

TOO LATE

139. This pain that dwells deep in my soul has paralyzed me, and will haunt me eternally. I just can't escape no matter what I do or where I go. I feel like its too late for me, like I have been left behind. I have spent too many years in pain, after a while it starts to take a toll on you. I feel like a soldier who has been wounded, that can no longer mount up the strength to move forward. Just let me die.

CURSED

140. I am blessed, but at the same time cursed. Where ever I go the devil is right behind me. It feels like death, pain, suffering, and trouble are stalking me. Where can I run to? Who can I confide in? I feel like I am trapped in a maze, constantly trying to avoid running into a dead end. Sometimes I ask myself "why me". No matter how good things start getting something always causes disaster. It seems like this happens everywhere I go and won't stop.

A DIFFERENT WORLD

141. Me and the homies, my homie girl and her friend went to south beach last night, and it seemed like a whole different world down there. It was completely different from how the hood is. People were dressed up, looking fancy, and having a good time. I felt out of pocket down there because I was broke and came from the hood. I would feel the same way if I was in Compton and went to Hollywood. I get a weird feeling when I go to these lavish styled places. It feels like I am on a different planet. That lets me know that the world has much more to offer me and my people. Sometimes I feel like

142. I have been restricted from the world outside of the ghetto. What is really fucked up is that I spent at least ten years living in Florida, but last night you would of thought that I was from out of town. The whole time that we were down there I kept thinking " damn, look how nice it is down here".

KIDS

143. God willing I hope I get a chance to have kids. I would like to have a daughter. Women are so beautiful that I must have one that I can say I made. I know that me and my baby girl will be so close that death won't be able to separate us. I love kids, I look at them as our second chance. They remind me of the innocence that I possessed a long time ago. I find comfort in their eyes, touch, and smell. They are very very precious to me.

RUTHLESS

144. There have been moments when I have done cynical things and did not have any remorse afterwards. I made up my mind a long time ago, so when I get into a confrontation or conflict my first thought is "its on". Survival is a human instinct, so off instinct my first thought is to engage in combat. The streets have become battlefields, and our homes have become command posts. In order to survive one must adapt him or herself to whatever circumstances that evolve around them. All I did was adapt.

NIGHTMARE

145. A couple of days ago I had a nightmare that I can't stop thinking about. All I can remember is me running from someone that was shooting at me. I tried to run as fast as I could, but the more I tried to run the slower I ran. The person I was running from caught up to me and shot me in the neck. I laid on the concrete squirming, gripping my neck, choking on my own blood. After I regained my conscience and realized that it was just a dream I didn't want to go back to sleep.

MONEY

146. The root of all evil! That dollar bill is so mighty that it can swallow your soul, if you let it. Money has become a plague to this world. It has destroyed millions of lives and caused massive destruction and mayhem. All this striving we do to get money. When we finally get it was it worth it? Does it help us or hurt us? I won't let it consume me, don't let it consume you.

LOVE

147. We have too much hate in this world. We have too much hate in our hearts. Fear and hate have consumed this world, and our hearts. We should try letting all of our fears and hate go, and start loving each other and loving life. First we must love ourselves in order to love someone else. Love can make a big difference in all of our lives. The side effects of love are the hurtful feelings of being betrayed, deceived, and used. No matter what never stop loving, because love heals.

I AM

148. I am a leader, I am a man, I am a lost soul seeking the promised land. I am a hideous scar that no one can bare to look at and cannot be healed. I am the vivid picture that is still, yet real. I am the cold eyes that stare without concern or care. I am the child that has abandoned his innocence. I am the good and the evil, the angel and the demon.

SHADOW

149. I used shadow as a break dancing name when I was younger. I can't remember why, I was into video games and other childish things at the time. Somehow I was intrigued by the name. Shadow eventually became my street name, evolving into my gang moniker. Shadow to me is a laid back behind the scenes individual. Very quiet but very dangerous.

LOOKS ARE DECEIVING

150. What an individual wears or how they speak doesn't really project who they are. One must go beyond the flesh to fully understand and get to know an individual. Humans (not all) tend to prejudge each other out of curiosity, not knowing that curiosity killed the cat. We must search deep to find the truth. We miss out on enjoying and learning from really great people by being so judgmental. I have surprised a lot of people that I have gotten to meet on my journey. Lets not be so defensive and learn to keep an open mind.

A NORMAL MAN

151. I don't know any normal men, I don't know any normal people to be honest. I do know that I love women and I love being in their presence. They are smart and sometimes naive, but never the less they are very complex and well designed. I don't know if a normal man notices all that, but I do. I like to study women, they get nothing but love from me, that's on everything.

CONSEQUENCES

152. There are good and bad consequences. The good ones we can triumph, and the bad ones we just have to deal with and learn from. Even doing the right thing has consequences, especially in a world where injustice rules. That doesn't mean we shouldn't do the right thing, it just means we have to be fully aware of the consequences of our actions. Telling the truth can get you killed, while lying can get you off the hook. Being real makes people despise you, while being fake helps you fit in. See what I mean?

DIVIDE AND CONQUER

153. We blacks cannot stick together because we have been taught at young ages to hate each other. My generation especially has forgotten what it means to be black. Family is very important to me, and I believe that there is nothing stronger than a close knit family. Blacks must look at each other as family and not enemies. We have been taught to hate ourselves, therefore we hate everyone that looks similar to us. Once we open our eyes and learn to love ourselves we will be able to see that "black is beautiful!"

DO OR DIE

154. This system that man, specifically the white man has designed gives young black males two options, do or die! They force us into a corner then make us feel trapped so we can panic and do something out of anger and fear. Don't force us to do something, help us do something! Until we receive the help that we need this world will without a doubt be terrorized day in and day out!

DAYS OF OUR LIVES

155. Everyday that me and my homies were together we stuck by each other, day in and day out. We were and are still so close that death cannot separate us. We had our ups and downs, and fall outs, but through and through we stayed true to each other. Even though psycko faded away a lot we all still loved him too. We did a lot together, a lot of good and bad. I don't know how my life will turn out, but good or bad, triumph or tragedy, I will stay true to my brothers from different mothers. That's on my soul.

FUCK ALL YALL!

156. This whole world and everything in it can kiss my black ass! People walk around like the world belongs to them, and nobody else matters. You muthafuckas are so selfish its a crying shame. I don't respect those who don't respect and acknowledge others. I acknowledge the potential and good in others but get overlooked by those same people! That is why I have decided to not give a fuck about how they feel or what they think. Fuck them all, and their feelings and opinions!

DEMONS

157. One night me and the homies were listening to some instrumentals. The music was so soothing that I closed my eyes. When I closed my eyes I started seeing demons hovering around me. To me that means the devil is notifying me that he is after my soul. He wants me to know that every move I make he will be right behind me, and if I slip and do what he wants I will be on a one way ticket straight to hell! Ain't that a bitch!

LIFE I LEAD

158. This life that I am living is starting to take a toll on me. Through all the pain and rain I must maintain. Its rough out here, and there is not a drop of pity or mercy in the air. These killing fields that I roam through are merciless. These dark streets show no sign of hope. Yet and still I strive to live a humble and appreciative life. If I think positive and stay determined things will change for the better.

SMILES AND CRIES

159. Do not let nothing stop you from smiling, and do not let nothing make you cry. When I say this I am saying do not let anything or anyone control you and your emotions. We give too much power to things and people, then wonder why we never get to where we want to be, or feel how we want to feel. Stop letting people and things control your life. You won't be able to live until you break free from anything or anyone that has control over your thoughts, actions, and lifestyle.

LET GO

160. God will not let me go. He is going to make me
endure this pain so that he can put me on display
for the whole world to see with their own eyes how
powerful he is, and that he is real. My life was suppose
to be over a long time ago. I gave up on life, but god
didn't give up on me. He understood what my struggle
was all about when I didn't have a clue. My purpose
was too deep for me to grasp on to and understand.
That's why I had such a rough life. Thank you father
for your grace and mercy.

SOMETHING ABOUT ME

161. There is something about me that makes people acknowledge me, and want to kill me. I doubt its my demeanor even though sometimes that is what it feels like it is. There is something about me that is deeper than the flesh, something not easy to explain. The way people watch me or look at me gives me the impression that I am of importance. The way people try not to acknowledge me is funny to me. Their actions speak louder than their words. A lot of these people are beneath me and know it but refuse to admit it. Just accept it, you ain't shit compared to me.

FEAR ONLY GOD

162. I am letting all my fears go, the only one I fear is god. I learned to conquer my fears a long time ago. I noticed that people tend to feed off of fear. If they can instill fear into you they can control you. The media does this a lot, make you believe in shit that isn't real. Manipulation and control give people a sense of power and dignity. Muthafuckas be power tripping! They have to control something or someone to feel important, or have some type of self worth. What a pity, with all that power you still ain't shit.

THICKER THAN WATER

163. Snipah is my brother and best friend, and he always will be for the rest of my life. We made a pact and shared a bond with each other. On Piru and beyond Piru, I will always be there for him like he was there for me. He has been taken in for murder, but has not been charged yet. We are so close that death cannot separate us! However long he has to do we are going to do it together. That's on my soul!

WHAT IS IT IN ME

164. What is it in me that makes me want to destroy things, and people? It seems like my destructive ways are natural. When I was an adolescent I was somewhat attracted and intrigued by the sight of burning flames. I use to set whatever I could on fire and watch it burn. I would become mesmerized just by watching things burn. It might sound crazy, but in a way I like being evil. It gives me a rush that I cannot explain.

CAN'T TURN BACK

165. I've been through too much to try and make a complete change. I will grow and prosper, but I will never become a whole different person. I don't believe I have to. I am not a bad person, I was just lost and confused for a very long time because I was taught wrong. We all have the power to turn negative into positive. That is what I am trying to do with my life. I don't plan on turning back, I am moving forward.

IF YOU ONLY KNEW

166. We humans have become too naive. We refuse to see the truth because the truth hurts. Instead we choose to use assumptions and rumors to guide us. We are lost, and trapped! The truth can get you killed, that is a risk I am willing to take. I have to fulfill my destiny, fate awaits me. I'd rather die knowing the truth than continue living a lie. This barely making it, poverty stricken, ignorant, foolish, selfish, and judgmental lifestyle that they have given us is not enough for me. I refuse to accept it. There is much more for us out there.

CRUSHED

167. My quick reactions have hurt a lot of peoples feelings. Sometimes I notice my actions and try to rectify my mistakes. On the other hand I am just ruthless and can't accept that I am wrong. I apologize to everyone that I have hurt. I tend to take my pain, anger, and frustration out on the wrong people, my people. I know that I must push this energy in a different direction, and use it to help me do something great.

PAST LIFE

168. I wonder what I was like in my past life? I know for a fact I was someone of great importance. Everyone's past makes their future. My past self would be ashamed to claim this generation. I am ashamed to claim this generation. How we live and operate disgusts me! Technology has made us lazy, we don't even use our brains half of the time. The children act like adults, while the adults act like children. Everything is backwards. This is probably why I am having such a difficult time in my present life.

TRANSFORMATION

169. I believe that now is the time to place my rightful place among kings and queens. This is my transformation from gang member and street scholar to new generation revolutionary, philosopher, and divine black leader. This whole time I was a caterpillar growing into a butterfly. The pain strengthened me and taught me valuable lessons. I couldn't see that in the process, but now its becoming clear to me that this must take place in order for me to grow and become who god intended me to be.

GIFT OF SPEECH

170. There is a side of me that wants to stay silent and destroy everything that I possibly can, but there is another side of me that has the gift of speech and can reach and motivate people. When I speak my words come from the soul, that is why I make such a big impact in society and peoples lives. I believe in myself, therefore when I come in contact with other people they will believe in me too. There will be a lot of people that won't take heed to my words. For those of you who do may god be with you.

SPIRITUAL

171. There are a lot of things that are just mind boggling to me. There are times when I can feel my spirit come out of my body. There are things that I see, feel, and hear that other people don't. A lot of people say "your crazy" and I reply " I know, I get that a lot". There is an unseen spiritual realm that exists that most people don't believe in because they cannot see it. There are things that we can feel but don't see, these things are spiritual. Like death for instance, you can feel it coming but don't see it until it has come and gone. Don't just pay attention to the natural, take heed to the spiritual things as well.

CROOKED ASS MUTHAFUCKAS

172. I hate crooked, bitch ass, little dick pigs! Yes I am talking about the police that terrorize black communities and instill fear into my people. There have been numerous occasions when the police have shot and killed people, and have only been suspended for a couple of weeks. A brother shoots and kills someone, he has his whole life taken from him. The police in my neighborhood sell drugs, rob, shoot, and kill people. I am one of the few people that don't fear police. They are my number one enemy. All we do with pigs is make bacon.

SO MUCH PAIN

173. I have lived a very painful life, and I have seen things that will make you scream to the top of your lungs. As a child I was murdered, emotionally. I was the type of kid that needed special attention. I never had a father so that left an empty space in my life. If I would have had a father I would of felt complete and whole, but since I didn't have a father I didn't know how to feel or what to think. I've spent almost my whole life feeling lost. It really really hurts to feel this way.

AS CLOSE AS YOU'LL GET

174. Reading my book will be as close as some people will get to me. There are a lot of things that are hard to speak on, so I just write it down. I'd rather write than speak anyway, since a lot of people do not comprehend spoken words. Some understand more when they read, and take the time to understand what they are reading. Some people are just idiots and don't want to understand, but there are a lot of people who look at things in a different perspective when they read. Seems like they receive a better understanding when something is written down instead of spoken.

FLASHBACKS

175. Right after my homie told me that he murdered somebody I got high and started having flashbacks of all the things that we did together. The memories were coming so fast I could barely keep up. I will never forget his smile. He had the type of smile that could brighten up your day. When I closed my eyes all I could see was fun and crazy memories zooming by. I love my homie very much, and I really miss him.

ONE BLOOD

176. Even though I have friends and family there are times when I feel like I have to face the whole world by myself. There are also times when I just feel all alone, that's a horrible feeling. I have had enough heart to roam and get lost, but I always find my way back. Being a leader is just in my nature. Whatever I believe in I am going to stand up for, deep or solo. I am going to be a blood until I die!

MONSTERS

177. We creep and crawl through the night, causing terror and bringing fright. Our thoughts are more cynical than a mental patients, and our lives are more horrifying than a Steven Spielberg film. Concealed by the darkness that we roam through. Fueled by hate, and evil as can be. Our minds dwell in a pit filled with grotesque and unimaginable beings. Our only purpose is to destroy.

FOLLOW YOUR DREAMS

178. Never give up, and never stop. Your dreams are all you have, until they come true. It is up to you whether or not you turn your dreams into reality. No matter what circumstances your under, or what condition your in, follow your dreams. As long as you are alive you can accomplish anything you work hard at. Everyone in this world has the potential to do anything they want to do. Let god guide you and help you achieve what you desire. You will never fail with him on your side, trust me.

LIKE A MOVIE

179. Mi vida loca! There have been moments in my life that feel like a writers movie script. Some things add up, and some things cannot be explained. Even though my life feels like a movie it is not a movie, its all real. I find myself reflecting on my past a lot, and thinking " damn that was a trip". When an episode is taking place it doesn't seem to have as much effect as when you rewind and look back at it. I look back on my past a lot and learn from it. You can too.

FOREVER IN MY HEART

180. My mother, the number one woman in my life has struggled just as much as I have. She still gets up everyday and lives her life. She has done the best that she can possibly do. My mother and every single black mother deserves an award for their hard work and dedication. I am sincerely sorry for all the stress and pain that I caused my mother to feel. I appreciate my mother for conceiving me and helping me grow. We act like twins instead of mother and son. My mother is a black queen, and a jewel that I will love and cherish for the rest of my life. To my mother Lisa, you will always be in my heart. Love JuJu

NOTHING TO BE PLAYED WITH

181. Man, this ghetto life is nothing to be played with. I feel like a Vietnam veteran. My mind and body is tired and weary. I am shell shocked, and haunted by paranoia. My life is a nightmare that I can't wake up from. Imagine walking around with a target are your back, that's how I feel most of the time. Everyone that I have loved I have lost. This isn't how my life is suppose to be, but unfortunately this is the way it is.

ETERNAL

182. I will never die, my spirit will live on until the end of time. If you believe that, you can live forever too. I am not afraid of death, because death cannot stop what god has planned for me. If you pay close attention you will see that even in death a lot of peoples legacy still lives on. Perfect example is Jesus Christ, his teachings are still taught and helping save souls til this day! You can be eternal if you truly stick to what you believe in.

IT DON'T STOP

183. No matter what happens in life never stop moving forward, because even if you stop the world won't, it will just keep rotating. Pray for the strength to fight until your dying day. Understand what you are fighting for and how important it is, and you will never stop fighting. Life is a war that must be fought continually. Also teach the next generation how to fight and endure. Help them understand what they are fighting for.

LOSS OF WORDS

184. What can you say to your homies family when they get locked up or killed? I was completely overwhelmed after I was separated from my homies. It drained me completely. I was devastated knowing that we would never be together again. After so much loss in my life I felt like that was the final blow. I couldn't even function half of the time. We had created a bond that I thought would never be broken, but was. I sunk even deeper into depression after that. I felt like I had died.

MY NIGGAZ

185. Snipah and psycko, my muthafuckin niggaz! I love you niggaz with all my heart. I can't believe all the shit that we have been through, good and bad. Kicking it everyday, smoked out, drunk like a muthafucka! These are the days of our lives. Til death do us part I'll hold our bond in my heart. Whoop!

BLACK PRINCE

186. To all my young black males who have been lead astray and brainwashed into thinking that we are gangsters and thugs, and that's all that we will ever be, that is a lie! Know your true identity my brother, you young black males are princes, destined to be kings! We have been robbed and deceived. We must rise and conquer this land like we did years ago. Once upon a time we were the rulers and kings of this land, that is what they don't want you to know. My brother you must strive to live a humble and righteous life. Lies and lust have damaged the black man, and young black male. Learn and prosper black prince, the world is yours.

NO REMORSE

187. I must go to the extreme to get my point across. I do not have mercy or pity for anyone. Life is do or die where I am from. Your either strong or weak, victim or warrior. I believe I have done and will continue to do what I have to do. What is done is done, I cannot look back, I can only move forward. We waste too much time on regret, some shit is just meant to be. There will be things that you are going to have to do that you don't want to do. People you love that you are going to have to separate yourself from. My attitude is "fuck it" I did what I had to do.

STREET SCHOLAR

188. I learned a lot kicking up dust. I have seen a lot and done a lot. People have used drugs around me all my life. I have seen people get stabbed, beaten, and shot in the street. The most important thing to know about the streets is that the streets are scandalous! Anything goes in the street, there are no rules and regulations. The streets will always be, its us the people who have to change.

DO THE RIGHT THING

189. Why do wrong when you can do right? I think the objective of life is to fulfill your purpose and complete your destiny. I strive to do the right thing. In the course of doing the right thing I end up doing the wrong thing, but that's my learning process. Whenever you get the opportunity to do something right do it! We must convert all our negatives into positives. No matter how much bad decisions you have made in your life as long as you are alive and able you can choose to do the right thing.

THANK YOU'S

190. First of all I want to thank my heavenly father god for giving me the idea to tell my story and for making this possible. I also want to thank Jesus Christ for giving up his life for our sins and being a great teacher and leader of our fathers word. I also want to thank my wife for being by my side when it seemed like we weren't going to make it. Thank you to my mother for enduring my struggle with me, and always loving me no matter what. Thank you to pops for your encouraging words and love in my time of need. Thank you to my son for being my world, it is because of you that I never gave up and continue to move forward today. I love you always and forever my

young black prince. Thank you to my aunt tootch for her unconditional love and support. Thank you to my sister dianya for being there for me during my lowest, I love you sis. Thank you to Jiwe author of " War of the bloods in my veins" and Sanyika Shakur author of " Monster, the autobiography of an L.A. Gang member" for having the courage to tell your story and inspire the next generation of bangers to take the negative and use it as positive. I read both of your books, and it inspired me to tell my story and reach out to those who understand where I am coming from, and those who don't. Thank you to Afeni Shakur, Tupac Shakur, Assata shakur, 191. Mutulu Shakur, Geronimo pratt, and countless others for your courage to stand up and fight for our people. Your legacy's will live on forever. Thank you to Tookie williams for helping me ultimately make the change that has helped me become the man I am today. Thank you to T rodgers from the black p stones for helping me understand what being a real blood means, and for helping all of us who were lost find our way. Thank you to bone from Athens/black p stone bloods for his documentary "bastards of the party", and for giving me more insight on how I can become a better leader. Thank you to the very few of you that truly had my back, and the many suckas that tried to keep me from fulfilling my purpose and reaching my destiny.

Made in the USA
Columbia, SC
20 February 2021